INTO THE MIST

INTO THE MIST

THE STORY OF THE EMPRESS OF IRELAND

ANNE RENAUD

DUNDURN PRESS
TORONTO

Copy Editor: Cheryl Hawley
Design: Jesse Hooper
Printer: Webcom

Library and Archives Canada Cataloguing in Publication

Renaud, Anne, 1957-
    Into the mist : The story of the Empress of Ireland / by Anne Renaud.

Includes bibliographical references and index.
Issued also in an electronic format.
ISBN 978-1-55488-759-0

    1. Empress of Ireland (Steamship)--Juvenile literature.
2. Shipwrecks--Québec (Province)--Saint Lawrence River
Estuary--Juvenile literature. I. Title.

G530.E4R46 2010   j910.9163'44   C2010-902674-8

1   2   3   4   5   14   13   12   11   10

  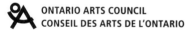

We acknowledge the support of the **Canada Council for the Arts** and the **Ontario Arts Council** for our publishing program. We also acknowledge the financial support of the **Government of Canada** through the **Canada Book Fund** and **Livres Canada Books**, and the **Government of Ontario** through the **Ontario Book Publishers Tax Credit program**, and the **Ontario Media Development Corporation**.

Care has been taken to trace the ownership of copyright material used in this book. The author and the publisher welcome any information enabling them to rectify any references or credits in subsequent editions.

J. Kirk Howard, President

The author acknowledges the support of the Canada Council for the Arts, which last year invested $20.1 million in writing and publishing throughout Canada.

Printed and bound in Canada.
www.dundurn.com

Dundurn Press
3 Church Street, Suite 500
Toronto, Ontario, Canada
M5E 1M2

Gazelle Book Services Limited
White Cross Mills
High Town, Lancaster, England
LA1 4XS

Dundurn Press
2250 Military Road
Tonawanda, NY
U.S.A. 14150

CONTENTS

In memory of those who once walked the decks of the *Empress of Ireland*

ACKNOWLEDGEMENTS

I extend heartfelt gratitude to my first readers, David St-Pierre, Derek Grout, David Zeni, and Jo-Anne Colby, who most graciously provided their time, expertise, and visual elements, which were instrumental in the realization of this book. I am also indebted to Marion Kelch, chair of the *Empress of Ireland* Artifacts Committee, as well as to my "contributors" whose ancestors sailed aboard the *Empress*, and who generously shared the rich pages of their family histories with me. Photographic contributions from the *Site historique maritime de la Pointe-au-Père* were substantial, and should also be noted.

INTRODUCTION

From 1906 to 1914, the *Empress of Ireland*, one of the fastest and most elegant liners of the Edwardian era, graced the waters of the Atlantic. During her many crossings between Canada and England, she ferried royals and inventors, authors and scientists, actors and politicians. But most importantly, she carried more than 115,000 hopeful immigrants who had left Europe to build their lives on Canadian soil. This is the story of the *Empress*, of the many people who walked her decks, and how, in the early morning hours of May 29, 1914, she came to rest on the bottom of the St. Lawrence River.

Canadian Pacific Archives (NS 3293)

Immigrants arriving at Quebec City.

THE CANADIAN PACIFIC RAILWAY

The Dominion of Canada was just 13 years old when the Canadian Pacific Railway was created in 1881.

A decade earlier, the province of British Columbia had joined Canada after Prime Minister Sir John A. Macdonald promised to build a transcontinental railway that would link the new western province to the provinces in the east within 10 years. The government hired a contractor named Andrew Onderdonk to begin construction of the railway from British Columbia, moving eastward. But because the Fraser Canyon was so treacherous, only a few kilometres of rail had been laid by 1881, and no work had begun on the railway from Ontario heading westward.

Glenbow Archives NA-1375-1

Sir John A. Macdonald was Canada's first prime minister. He served from 1867 to 1873, and again from 1878 to 1891.

Canadian Pacific Archives (NS 13561-2)

Track construction in the lower Fraser Valley of British Columbia in 1883.

TIME CAPSULE

The Canadian Pacific Railway was created by a group of Canadian businessmen who invested their money and obtained funds and land from the government to build a railway linking Canada from coast to coast. The company was incorporated on February 16, 1881.

For British Columbia to remain a part of the country the prime minister had to keep his promise, and time was running out.

It was up to the newly founded Canadian Pacific Railway — or CPR — to bind Canada from coast to coast with a ribbon of steel.

The Canadian government gave the company $25 million and 25 million acres of land to build the railway. Over the next four years, across mountain ranges, lakes, rivers, and forests, the CPR oversaw Canada's largest railway-building project, under the watchful eye of William Cornelius Van Horne.

Once the country was linked from east to west, the Canadian government had to find settlers to fill the wide expanses of land that lay in between. The owners of the CPR also had to find passengers to fill the seats aboard the trains that were now panting their way across the country. Newcomers in search of affordable farmland would provide a common solution.

In the 1890s, both the CPR and the Canadian government sent agents to Europe to encourage people to come and develop the Canadian West. They placed advertisements in European newspapers and magazines and distributed posters and pamphlets.

TIME CAPSULE

Andrew Onderdonk supervised the building of the railway through the most difficult stretch in the entire route, from Port Moody to Eagle Pass in British Columbia. Between 1880 and 1885, many thousands of men, including 8,000 Chinese labourers, carried out the perilous work of clearing the land, dynamiting the rock, building trestles and bridges, and laying 545 kilometres of track. There were numerous accidents and many workers died and were buried alongside the rails. Among those who lost their lives were hundreds of Chinese workers, who were often given the most dangerous tasks.

Library and Archives Canada (C-008549)

William Cornelius Van Horne became general manager of the CPR in 1882, and was the driving force behind the completion of the railway's transcontinental main line less than four years later.

Canadian Pacific Railway Bridge.

Government programs offered immigrants reduced fares on ships and provided them with farmland and equipment at low cost once they arrived in Canada. Although English-speaking immigrants, such as people from Britain, were preferred, settlers from northern and central Europe who were willing to become farmers were also welcomed.

Poster to attract settlers to Canada.

But transporting people on land was only one of the CPR's many goals. The oceans were the next challenge. By 1887, the company had purchased its first steamships, which transported people and cargo across the Pacific, to and from Japan and China.

Building the Canadian Pacific Railway through Kicking Horse Pass, on the border of Alberta and British Columbia.

Soon the company set its sights on another goal — a contract for the delivery of British mail to Japan and China, via Canada.

TIME CAPSULE

On November 7, 1885, Donald A. Smith hammered the last iron spike into the railway, at Craigellachie, British Columbia, near Eagle Pass. The track from the west was now officially joined with the track from the east. On June 28, 1886, less than a year later, the first passenger train to complete the transcontinental trip left Montreal. By the time it reached Port Moody, British Columbia, on July 4, it had covered nearly 4,700 kilometres of rail in five days and 19 hours.

Glenbow Archives NA-1494-5

Driving the last spike on the Canadian Pacific Railway, Craigellachie, British Columbia.

However, for the company to deliver the mail within the strict time limits required by such a contract, it needed ships that were much faster than the ones it already had.

To solve this problem, the CPR ordered the first three ships in its fleet of *Empresses* to be built. Nicknamed the "Flying Empresses" because of their speed and elegance, the *Empress of India*, the *Empress of China*, and the *Empress of Japan* began providing quick delivery of the mail across the Pacific Ocean in 1891. The mail from Britain travelled across Canada to Vancouver by train, then onward to Asia by ship. This route was reversed for mail travelling from China and Japan, destined for Britain.

With the success of these first three ships, the CPR was convinced it would soon be awarded the mail contract for the Atlantic Ocean. But to deliver the mail between England and Canada on time, the company needed to add more speedy ships to its fleet.

And so began the story of the *Empress of Ireland*.

In the 1880s, immigrants travelled by train to Western Canada.

Provincial Archives of Manitoba (N 7934)

A LUXURIOUS LINER

In December 1904, Sir Thomas George Shaughnessy, president of the Canadian Pacific Railway, placed an order for the building of the two *Empress* ships intended for the Atlantic. The contract was awarded to the Fairfield Shipbuilding and Engineering Company.

The sister ships, almost identical in outward appearance and interior furnishings, were built in just over a year in one of the massive shipyards on the River Clyde by Glasgow, Scotland. They were christened the *Empress of Britain* and the *Empress of Ireland*.

From bow to stern, the *Empress of Ireland* measured 173.7 metres — almost the length of two football fields — and she was 20 metres across at her widest point. From her keel to her top deck she measured 26.5 metres, the height of an eight-storey building. Her maximum speed was 20 knots, about 37 kilometres per hour.

The *Empress* could carry approximately 1,550 passengers, in three classes. First-class tickets were the most expensive, because first-class cabins and facilities were on

An ad for the Fairfield Shipbuilding and Engineering Company, Ltd.

the ship's highest decks, where sunlight and fresh air were most abundant. Second- and third-class passengers were housed on the ship's lower decks.

The higher decks were also more ornate and richly decorated, with furnishings of plush velvet and taffeta, expensive leathers, and thick carpets. The panelling and carvings were made from costly woods such as oak, mahogany, and teak.

Third-class dining room.

Second-class dining room.

First-class dining room.

Children's first-class dining room. Children who travelled in first class had their own dining room, while children of second- and third-class passengers ate with their parents.

First-class dining room.

David St-Pierre Collection

All totalled, the *Empress* had eight decks, or levels. From the bottom moving upward, the ship's three lowest decks were the Orlop Deck, the Lower Deck, and the Main Deck, home to the third-class dining room and some of the third-class passengers' cabins.

Above them sat the Upper Deck and the Shelter Deck. They included the living quarters of many of the crew members, the cabins for second-class passengers, the first-class barbershop, the galleys, and the hospital, where the ship's doctor and nurses cared for sick passengers. These decks also housed the first- and second-class dining rooms for adults, the first-class dining room for children, and the third-class children's playground.

Courtesy of the Peabody Essex Museum

Third-class children's playground.

A first-class cabin.

David St-Pierre Collection

The following two decks were the Lower Promenade and Upper Promenade. These housed many luxurious first-class facilities, including the library, the smoking lounge, the café, the bar, and the music room, as well as recessed areas where passengers could lounge in deckchairs and enjoy the sea breezes.

Finally came the Boat Deck, the ship's top level, where most of the lifeboats were stowed. The navigational bridge, where the captain and officers gave the orders to steer the ship, was also perched here.

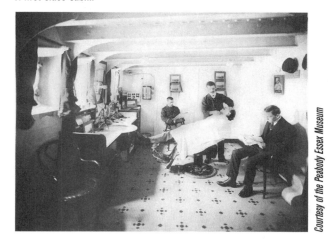

First-class barbershop.

Courtesy of the Peabody Essex Museum

First-class library.

David St-Pierre Collection

Main staircase leading from first-class cabins on the Upper and Lower Promenade Decks to the dining room on Shelter Deck.

David St-Pierre Collection

The *Empress of Ireland* was launched on January 27, 1906, and for several months thereafter remained in the builder's shipyard while a team of craftsmen, including carpenters, plumbers, and electricians, completed her interior furnishings. By the time the liner was ready for her first ocean crossing, the Canadian Pacific Railway had secured its second mail contract, to deliver the mail to and from Britain across the Atlantic Ocean.

The CPR was not only delivering mail from Liverpool to Hong Kong, but was also transporting passengers across vast distances, almost circling the globe. For the first time, people could step on a ship in England, cross the Atlantic to Canada, board a train that would carry them across the country to the West Coast, then board another ship that would bring them to China, all within the same company network of ships and trains.

The Sphere, May 29, 1909

The extent of the Canadian Pacific system: Liverpool to Hong Kong. 19,056 kilometres.

Immigrants aboard the *Empress of Ireland*.

Site historique maritime de Pointe-au-Père Collection

3 BON VOYAGE

O n June 29, 1906, the *Empress of Ireland* set out on her maiden voyage from Liverpool, England, for Quebec City. She carried 1,276 passengers and more than 400 crew members. By late afternoon on July 6, the liner had reached Pointe-au-Père, a small patch of land 300 kilometres downstream from the port of Quebec,

TIME CAPSULE

In 1891, William Cornelius Van Horne designed the CPR's checkered flag logo, which was soon flown by all its ships. He explained that he chose this flag because it was different from other designs and was easy to recognize when it hung loose. Some people believe it was inspired by the contract the company had signed with the Canadian government to build the transcontinental railway. On the map of the proposed railway, the land on either side of the track was identified by a patchwork of alternating red and white squares. The red squares represented pieces of land that would remain the property of the Canadian government, while the white squares identified land granted to the company to build the railway.

TIME CAPSULE

Depending on the weather, in particular the presence of fog on the St. Lawrence River, it usually took the *Empress* six to seven days to travel the 4,500 kilometres between England and Canada. However, the CPR's advertising posters boasted ONLY FOUR DAYS – OPEN SEA. This was to attract nervous passengers who were not fond of sailing on ocean waters. The four days were the time it took to sail from Tory Island, off the coast of Ireland, to Belle Isle, Newfoundland. The other sailing days were not considered to be "open sea" because they took place within the sheltered waters of the St. Lawrence River, in the 1,126-kilometre stretch that separates Quebec from the Atlantic.

Canadian Pacific Archives (A6352)

Empress Steamers advertising poster.

TIME CAPSULE

As the CPR's trains made their way across the country, portions of railway cars — and sometimes entire cars — were used as miniature post offices, in which postal workers busied themselves sorting, delivering, and picking up the mail. Because time was so crucial, these workers were often tested and graded on their speed and accuracy.

Interior of Canadian Pacific Railway mail car.

Glenbow Archives NA-1315-35

on which sat a lighthouse and the river pilot station. There, a small steamboat met the *Empress* so the river pilot could board the ship and guide her through the narrowing shores of the St. Lawrence River.

TIME CAPSULE

Located 50 kilometres downstream from Quebec City, the island of Grosse Île served as a quarantine station from 1832 to 1937. Ship passengers carrying diseases such as smallpox, measles, and cholera, which could be spread to others on the mainland, were kept on the island for a period of time, until they were healthy. During the Great Famine in Ireland (1845–49), thousands of Irish fled to Canada to avoid starvation and death. Already weak from hunger and illness when they boarded the ships, countless died at sea or shortly after arriving at Grosse Île. By the end of 1847, more than 5,000 Irish immigrants had been buried there.

A half-hour after she left Pointe-au-Père, another small steamboat met the *Empress* off Rimouski to collect the mailbags destined for Canada. These mailbags were later off-loaded onto trains in Rimouski for the sorting and delivery process to begin.

It was also there that CPR ticket agents boarded the *Empress* to supply passengers with railway tickets and to make sleeping car reservations through to their final destinations. Immigration, customs, and medical officials also came on board off Rimouski. As the *Empress* continued to make her way up river, doctors examined passengers to see if any needed to be quarantined at Grosse Île, while customs officials inspected their luggage and immigration officials made sure the newcomers had all the documents necessary to enter the country.

In the early hours of July 7, the *Empress* sailed into the port of Quebec City, where she was welcomed by hundreds of people anxious to get a glimpse of the elegant new ocean liner. Mailbags from England bound for Japan and China were quickly removed and loaded onto a special train that would speed them across the country. Returning Canadian residents left the ship and collected their luggage, while newcomers made their way to the immigration sheds to continue the process of becoming citizens in their new country.

By the afternoon of July 12, the *Empress* was ready to depart for Liverpool and complete her first round-trip ocean voyage. During her five days in port, the liner had been cleaned and inspected, her bed linens, napkins, and tablecloths had been laundered and ironed, and her galleys restocked with food. The mailbags from Japan and China, bound for England, had also been off-loaded from a special transcontinental train onto the ship.

Before the *Empress* reached the open sea, the pick-ups and drop-offs of a few days earlier were repeated in reverse. The mailbags from Canada, destined for England, were loaded onto the ship off Rimouski, and the river pilot who had guided the ship from the port of Quebec took his leave off Pointe-au-Père.

For the remainder of that spring and summer, the *Empress* continued her route between Liverpool and Quebec. When winter set in and she was no longer able to travel the St. Lawrence River because of ice and snow, the *Empress* changed her route, making the ports of Halifax, Nova Scotia, and Saint John, New Brunswick, her Canadian destinations.

> ## TIME CAPSULE
>
> Food supplies for a six-day crossing included:
>
> 10,800 eggs
> 4,400 kg of beef, lamb, veal, and pork
> 3,500 kg of flour
> 2,000 litres of milk and cream
> 1,000 kg of rice
> 1,000 kg of fresh fruit
> 250 kg of cheese
> 250 kg of sugar

When the trail of ice floes disappeared from the St. Lawrence River in the spring, the *Empress* once again took up her Liverpool–Quebec route. For the next eight years, the elegant liner mostly kept to this pattern of alternating ports.

 # EARLY CROSSINGS

After welcoming two new provinces, Alberta and Saskatchewan, in 1905, Canada counted a total of nine provinces and two territories, which were home to more than six million people. The country was growing rapidly. By 1907, its prairie landscapes were slowly being transformed by fields of wheat and other grains, and new towns such as Medicine Hat, Regina, and Brandon had sprouted alongside the new transcontinental railway.

Throughout these early years of the twentieth century, thousands of hopeful newcomers continued to board the *Empress of Ireland* and cross the Atlantic to forge a new life for themselves in Canada.

While many of them became farmers, other settlers took jobs as factory workers in cities such as Montreal and Toronto. As well, young women found employment as maids and nannies, while some men worked in remote areas, labouring in mines, lumber camps, and on the railroads. The *Empress* also brought several groups of "home children," many of them boys from the Fegan Homes.

TIME CAPSULE

British children who were orphaned, or whose parents were too poor or sick to care for them, were taken in by orphanages or "homes" such as the Fegan Homes and the Barnardo Homes. These children became known as "home children." Between 1869 and the 1930s, over 100,000 British "home children" were sent to Canada and other countries in the hope of a better life. In Canada, the children were placed with families, to work in exchange for food, shelter, a small allowance, and the opportunity to go to school. Boys usually helped out on the farm, while girls performed household chores.

Courtesy of Fegan Homes

Boys from Fegan Homes aboard the *Empress*.

Now and again, the ship's passenger lists included the names of travellers who would someday figure in world history books, if they did not already. One of these noteworthy passengers was John McCrae, who sailed on the *Empress* in October 1906, when he travelled from Quebec to take the Royal College of Physicians exams in London, England. John enjoyed his first sailing experience so much that he made the return trip aboard the liner as well, arriving on November 22 in Halifax, since the *Empress* had begun her winter sailings.

Other passengers included Sir Sandford Fleming, Rudyard Kipling, Guglielmo Marconi, and Sir Robert Baden-Powell, who, on July 29, 1910, boarded the *Empress* in Liverpool with 15 boy scouts for a cross-country visit of Canada. While aboard the ship, the scouts learned navigation and practised first aid.

Politicians and members of royal families also graced the decks of the *Empress*. Among them were Prince Fushimi of Japan; Canada's ninth and tenth governor generals, Lord Grey and the Duke of Connaught; and William Lyon Mackenzie King, who would become Canada's tenth prime minister in 1921.

"Empress of Ireland Waltz" sheet music.

TIME CAPSULE

Dubbed the "March Queen" by famous American conductor and composer John Philip Sousa, Myrtle C. Wallace (1870–1948) of Cambridge, Vermont, wrote more than fifty marches and other musical works during her lifetime. In 1908, Myrtle, also known as "Myrtie," composed the "Empress of Ireland Waltz," in honour of the ship.

TIME CAPSULE

Born and raised in Guelph, Ontario, John McCrae was a writer, doctor, teacher, and soldier. During The First World War he served as a doctor with the Canadian Army Medical Corps. While he was posted in Belgium, he witnessed many bloody battles. During that time he wrote a poem, "In Flanders Fields," which was published in a British magazine in December 1915. It soon came to symbolize the sacrifice of war. On Remembrance Day every year, millions of people wear a red poppy emblem, inspired from his poem, to honour those who died in combat.

John McCrae and his dog Bonneau.

Library and Archives Canada (C-046284)

Library and Archives Canada (PA-025748)

Sir Sandford Fleming.

TIME CAPSULE

Sandford Fleming immigrated to Canada from his native Scotland in 1845, at the age of 17. Among his many accomplishments, he designed Canada's first postage stamp, the Three-Penny Beaver, in 1851. In later years he surveyed the first rail route across Canada and was chief engineer for the Canadian Pacific Railway Company. He also developed and implemented the international system of standard time.

A stamp commemorating Guglielmo Marconi.

Guglielmo Marconi invented the wireless telegraph, which allowed people to send messages to each other over great distances. Some ships had a wireless telegraph office on board to communicate with the mainland and with other ships at sea.

In the 1890s, Robert Baden-Powell began teaching scouting to the young soldiers in his regiment. By 1907, he had founded the World Scout Movement. Today, the movement counts more than 38 million members worldwide.

TIME CAPSULE

Author Rudyard Kipling was born in Bombay, India, in 1865 and schooled in England. He began writing as a young man and had his first story published at age 18. Kipling travelled the world, and while he was living in the United States he wrote *The Jungle Book*, which became a children's classic. He received the Nobel Prize for Literature in 1907.

Courtesy of the Library of Congress, LC-DIG-ggbain-03724

Rudyard Kipling.

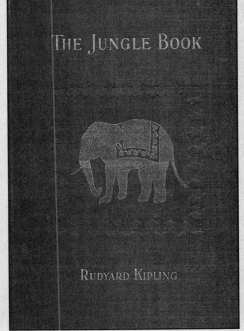

Author's Collection

The cover of the *Jungle Book*.

PASSENGER CHRONICLES

Winifred Ada Lawrence

Winifred Ada Lawrence was 11 years old when she boarded the *Empress* in Liverpool with her parents and seven brothers and sisters in March 1908. After a rough crossing, during which almost all the Lawrences were seasick, the family arrived at the port of Saint John, New Brunswick, then boarded a train for a long, rattling ride to the province of Quebec, and onward to Ontario.

Phil Grignon Collection

Winifred Ada Lawrence at age 20 in Barrie, Ontario.

After they settled in Barrie, Winifred's father found work taking care of the lawns and gardens of wealthy homeowners. As soon as she was old enough, Winifred also worked to help support the family. While still a teenager, she cooked and cleaned for a prominent Barrie family, the Ardaghs. At age 20, she married Louis Stanislas Grignon. In 1919, the couple moved to Ste-Agathe-des-Monts, Quebec, where they lived for 31 years, raising three sons. After her husband retired from his job at the post office, the Grignons moved back to Barrie, where they bought the very same house Winifred had lived in after her family settled in Canada. Winifred even returned to work as a maid for Mrs. Ardagh, who was then 95 years old!

Agnes Desideria Anderson

Agnes Desideria Anderson and her family lived on a farm in a little village in Sweden, just below the Arctic Circle. For many years, the country had suffered from over-population, which led to food shortages and limited job opportunities. Because of these problems, many Swedish people chose to leave. In late April 1910, five-year-old Agnes, along with her parents and four older brothers and sisters, said goodbye to their friends and relatives, and travelled for days by train and boat to Liverpool, England, where they boarded the *Empress* for Canada. Upon their arrival in Quebec on May 13, the family took the transcontinental train to Vancouver.

Mavis Nelson Collection

Agnes Desideria Anderson.

Throughout their five-day journey, Agnes's father bought food for the family whenever the train stopped. Some meals consisted of no more than cheese and crackers. During the day the family sat on wood benches, and at night Agnes and her brothers and sisters slept on the floor of the train. From Vancouver, the Andersons then made their way south to the state of Washington, where they lived for five years. In 1916, the family returned to Canada and settled on a farm in Falun, Alberta. Agnes later became a teacher and taught at different schools throughout Alberta. She often rode to and from school on horseback.

THE CRIPPEN CURSE

The year 1910 marked the halfway point of the *Empress of Ireland*'s eight-year sailing career. Who could have suspected the tragedy that would unfold in four year's time?

By then the *Empress* was woven into the life stories of thousands of people who had worked or sailed upon her decks. Oddly, that year she became linked to a man who would never set foot on the liner. He was a doctor named Hawley Harvey Crippen.

On July 20, 1910, Dr. Crippen and his sweetheart, Ethel Le Neve, boarded the Canadian Pacific ship *Montrose* in Antwerp, Belgium, bound for Canada.

Hawley Harvey Crippen.

Ethel Clara Le Neve.

Hawley Harvey Crippen and Ethel Le Neve.

The National Archives, ref. MEP03/198

The National Archives, ref. MEP03/198

Cora Crippen.

TIME CAPSULE

Henry George Kendall first went to sea at age 15 as a crew member aboard the *City of Berlin*. After working on a number of other ships, he was assigned to the *Empress of Ireland* as chief officer in 1907, then appointed captain of the *Montrose* in 1910. In May 1914, he rejoined the *Empress of Ireland*, this time as captain.

David St-Pierre Collection

Captain Henry George Kendall.

The two passengers travelled in disguise. Dr. Crippen posed as Mr. Robinson and Ethel Le Neve, dressed in boy's clothing, masqueraded as his teenage son, John Jr.

A few days before sailing, the commander of the *Montrose*, Captain Henry George Kendall, had read with interest a front-page newspaper article that described how the search of a London house by inspectors from Scotland Yard had led to the gruesome discovery of human remains. The residents of the house in question were Dr. Crippen and his wife, Cora. Dr. Crippen's wife had mysteriously disappeared in February of that year, and the remains were believed to be hers. Suddenly a prime suspect in Cora's murder, Dr. Crippen was thought to have fled London with his new girlfriend, Ethel Le Neve.

Before long, the couple drew the attention of Captain Kendall. Despite the fact that the newspaper photograph of Dr. Crippen showed a man wearing eyeglasses and the passenger who called himself Mr. Robinson did not wear any, Captain Kendall saw a clear resemblance between the two. The captain also noticed the telltale indentations on either side of Mr. Robinson's nose, where he suspected eyeglasses had once sat. Finally, Captain Kendall had read that Dr. Crippen had many gold fillings, so he invited the two passengers to have dinner with him. During the meal, the man who called himself Mr. Robinson laughed loudly, revealing a mouthful of gold-filled molars.

Canadian Pacific Archives (A-12894)

Dr. Crippen and Ethel Le Neve (disguised as a boy). This photo was taken by Captain Kendall aboard the *Montrose* the day before their arrest.

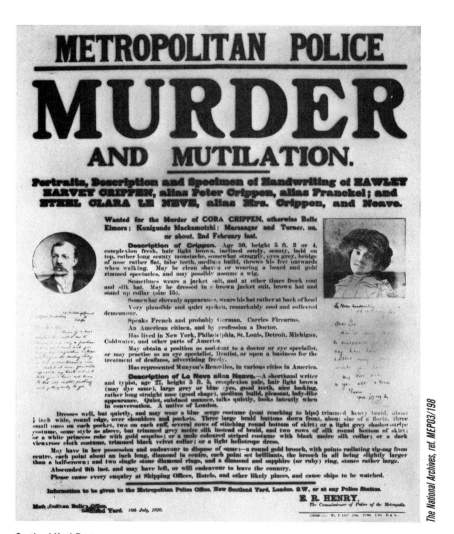

Scotland Yard Poster.

The captain decided to send a telegraph to Scotland Yard from the *Montrose* on July 22, to inform the authorities of his growing suspicions of the true identity of his passengers. Alerted by Captain Kendall's message, Inspector Walter Dew, who had been assigned to investigate the disappearance of Dr. Crippen's wife, made his way to Liverpool where he boarded the passenger ship *Laurentic* in pursuit of the couple.

The *Laurentic*.

Canadian Pacific Archives (A-12892)

The *Montrose* aboard which Dr. Crippen and Miss Le Neve were arrested at Point-au-Père..

Crippen and Le Neve remained unaware of the events that were taking place around them. All the while, newspapers on both sides of the Atlantic provided readers with a daily chronicle of the drama at sea as Inspector Dew raced towards Quebec aboard the speedy *Laurentic*.

Within days the *Laurentic* had overtaken the *Montrose*. Inspector Dew then telegraphed Captain Kendall from aboard the *Laurentic* informing him that he would be awaiting the arrival of the *Montrose* at Pointe-au-Père to nab the runaway couple. In the early hours of July 31, two days after the *Laurentic*'s arrival, a pilot boat met the *Montrose* at Pointe-au-Père. Disguised as a river pilot, Inspector Dew boarded the ship and made his arrests. It was the first time Guglielmo Marconi's invention of the wireless telegraph had been used to trap fugitives.

VOL. XLII. No. 175

Dr. Crippen and Le Neve Woman Are on Board of Montrose, Due At Quebec on Saturday Afternoon

Wireless Message from Montrose Received by Scotland Yard Saying Identification has been Confidently Established — Chief Inspector Dew, of Scotland Yard, in Pursuit on Board ¿S. Laurentic, and May Arrest Couple at Sea — Gaining on Montrose Three and a Half Miles Per Hour — Message from Montrose was Relayed from Sardinian, which Explains Mix-up Regarding Latter Vessel — Detailed Review of Case from Start to Present Time.

By Special Cable From Our Own Correspondent.

London, July 25.—The attention of all Europe is focussed on Canada, Interest in the Jeffries-Johnson fight was great here, but is entirely eclipsed by this morning's dramatic developments of the Crippen murder.

Never was an ocean race watched so keenly as that between the White Star steamer Laurentic, with Detective-Inspector Dew aboard, and the Montreal-Antwerp Canadian Pacific steamer Montrose, carrying the detective's prey, namely, Dr. Crippen, the alleged murderer of Mrs. Cora Crippen, and Miss Le Neve, his stenographer, disguised as an old gentleman and a boy, calling themselves Mr. and Master Robinson.

missing couple are published by Scotland Yard.

July 18.—A reward of $1,250 is offered for information that will lead to the arrest of Dr. Crippen and Ethel Clare Le Neve.

July 20.—Dr. Crippen and the Le Neve girl leave Antwerp for Canada as Mr. Robinson and son, aboard the SS. Montrose.

July 21 and 22.—Wireless message from Montrose saying that their identification has been confidently established.

July 22.—Chief Inspector Dew sails from Liverpool on board the Laurentic to arrest the fugitives in mid-ocean or on their arrival in Canada.

A MUCH-SOUGHT MAN

Dr. Crippen.

tives has been already decided, so far as Inspector Dew and the captain of the steamer are concerned.

LAURENTIC'S CAPTAIN PROMISES TO TRY AND

MANY DROWNED IN SUNDAY BOATING

Thirty-one Deaths Recorded in the States, Fatalities Either While Canoeing or Bathing.

Special to the Montreal Star.

New York, July 25.—Thirty-one persons, ten of whom were New Yorkers, were drowned on Sunday while either bathing or boating. New England equalled New York in the number of victims, having ten altogether.

Two bodies of persons drowned several days ago were cast up by the waves during the day. At Buffalo two girls lost their lives, and their two men companions saved themselves, when a squall overturned the canoe in which they were paddling.

The Harlem, East and Hudson rivers claimed some of the ten victims in New York. One of three bathers lost his life in Harlem river, while the other two were nearly drowned in their efforts to save him.

CLEVELAND'S GRANDFATHER

Ancestor of ex-President Sold to Montreal Resident.

Special to The Montreal Star.

Boston, Mass, July 25.—Miss Rose Cleveland, sister of the late Grover Cleveland, in her investigation of Cleveland genealogy finds that great-grandfather of Grover Cleveland, Richard Falley, was sold to a Montreal woman as a servant, for sixteen gallons of rum.

Richard Falley, Cleveland's great-grandfather, was born on the island of Guernsey. When ten years age he was kidnapped and taken to

TORONTO PAPER ASKS IF GOVERNMENT IS STRIKE-BREAKING

Alleges Federal Immigration Regulations Withdrawn Last Week, and Wants to Know Why.

Special to The Montreal Star.

Toronto, Ont., July 25.—The World to-day prints the following on its front page under heading "Is the Government strike-breaking":

"Did the Ottawa Government conspire with the Grand Trunk to weaken or break the strike by withdrawing the Federal regulation which prevents workmen who sign contracts in a foreign country, or men who have not $25 cash in their pocket, from entering Canada? Certainly these regulations were withdrawn last week. But the reason given was that it was for the purpose of showing men to come in to work on railway construction in the west.

"Those who make the charge say that when the strike seemed unavoidable, the Globe had a special item with a border about it and in its leading pages on its first page, dealing with this scarcity of men for railway construction, and Collingwood Schreiber, Government engineer in connection with the G. T. P. and the N. T. was given as the authority.

"On July 19th, another equally prominent item was published, dated Winnipeg, July 17th, saying that W. W. Corey, Deputy Minister of the Interior, was on his way to join Sir Wilfrid Laurier and Hon. Mr. Graham, Minister of Railways, and to confer with them on this question. The Department of the Interior had charge of the enforcement of the case against this kind of labor coming in. The conference took place in the west.

NORTI HU

Many To Near

Special Milan, taking by last Northern dred per property several smaller oblitera ging pr hundred Governo Amo hurrica Lonsale here, a of the covere

To

Another Exclusive Wireless From Captain Kendall

(Registered according to the Copyright Act.)

SS. Montrose, July 30, 1910.
Via Father Point, Que.

To the Editor of the Montreal Star.

I have received your wireless request. The supposed Crippen was on deck early, looking at Belle Isle. He had a worried look, and was pacing the deck like one in thought.

The supposed Miss Le Neve was in her room all day. She wears a gloomy expression.

We stopped in the fog last night.

The suspects said they did not sleep. Miss Le Neve does not smile or laugh. Both appear haggard.

I will send another wireless to-morrow.

((Signed) KENDALL,
Commander.

Montreal Daily Star, July 30, 1910.

ESTABLISHED 1764   QUEBEC. MONDAY. AUGUST

DR. CRIPPEN NOW PRISONER LONG CHASE HAS ENDED

Alleged Wife-Murderer and Miss Le Neve Arrested on the Steamer Montrose at Father Point Yesterday Morning.

The Bargain Baza
THE Big Bargain Bazaar Basement is attracti mense crowds every day. dreds of new bargains from e partment are rushed down Bazaar every morning and cl a mere fraction of the forme Come early Monday.

Quebec Chronicle, August 1, 1910.

Montreal Daily Star, August 1, 1910.

Wireless telegraph station at Point-au-Pière.

At the time of his arrest, the enraged Dr. Crippen cursed Captain Kendall for having turned him in. In 1914 the blight on the captain's head became known as the Crippen Curse, following the sinking of the *Empress of Ireland*, which had as its commander none other than Captain Henry George Kendall.

TIME CAPSULE

The lighthouse and pilot station at Pointe-au-Père have played an important role in Canada's maritime history. Four lighthouses were built here between 1859 and 1975, and a wireless telegraph station was added in 1909. Known as the Marconi Station, this was used to send and receive messages to and from ships at sea. Pointe-au-Père's third lighthouse, also built in 1909, is 33-metres high, making it one of the highest in Canada. It has been out of use since 1975, when it was replaced by an automated lighthouse. The following year it was designated a Canadian historic site to highlight its role in helping ships navigate the St. Lawrence River during the early years of the 20th century.

Site historique maritime de la Pointe-au-Père Collection

Lighthouse at Pointe-au-Père.

 # LATER CROSSINGS

By the end of 1911, the *Empress of Ireland* had crossed the Atlantic 132 times. On her trips eastward she had carried more than 46,000 passengers to England, while on her journeys westward she had ferried nearly 79,000 passengers, many of whom had created new lives for themselves in Canada.

During the crossings, passengers occupied their time by strolling on deck and chatting with new acquaintances. They read books, played card games, or wrote entries in their journals and letters to friends and family. On Sundays they attended church services. As each day unfolded, mealtimes were announced by the blare of a bugle, signalling to passengers to make their way to their respective dining rooms.

Evenings were often spent in the music rooms, which were each furnished with a piano. Some passengers even travelled with their own instruments, such as harmonicas, fiddles, and accordions, which they played to entertain each other.

All the while the ship's crew members, about 400 of them, carried out their respective duties. The captain and senior officers navigated the ship to bring her safely

First-class passengers reading on Upper Promenade Deck.

First-class passengers taking tea on Upper Promenade deck.

David St-Pierre Collection

David St-Pierre Collection

First-class passengers played games such as deck cricket, deck golf, or quoits, which involved throwing iron rings at a wooden stick to encircle it.

First-class passengers playing deck golf.

Third-class music room.

First-class music room.

CANADIAN PACIFIC RAILWAY COMPANY

R.M.S. "EMPRESS OF IRELAND.

THIRD CLASS

Breakfast.

Oatmeal Porridge
Stewed Steak & Onions
Irish Stew
Marmalade
Tea   Coffee

Dinner.

Bouilli Soup
Ragout of Veal
Roast Mutton, Onion Sauce
Parsnips   Boiled Potatoes
Semolina Pudding

Tea.

American Dry Hash
Cold—Roast Beef
Cheese   Pickles
Currant Buns   Bread & Butter
Preserves

Supper.

Gruel, Cabin Biscuits & Cheese

April 25, 1910.

Empress third-class menu.

to port, while electricians, plumbers, and engineers ensured her maintenance. In the galleys, butchers, cooks, and bakers prepared the thousands of meals served every day, after which scullions washed mounds of dishes and cutlery. Toiling in the heat and soot of the ship's engine and boiler rooms were the greasers, who oiled and greased the many moving parts of the ship's main engines, and the stokers, who fed the furnaces with coal to power the vessel. Throughout the ship, dozens of stewards and stewardesses tended to both passengers and senior officers, serving meals, making beds, cleaning cabins, and replenishing towels and linens. The ship's crew also held regular fire and safety drills and inspections.

Jean-Pierre Vallée Collection

Crew members, such as cabin boys, were often teenagers. They tended to the ship's senior officers. Their duties included running errands and bringing meals.

Stokers feeding coal into the furnace.

David St-Pierre Collection

The Titanic, *before she sank on her maiden voyage*

Courtesy of Derek Grout Collection

TITANIC TRAGEDY FULLY DESCRIBED
Pages Devoted to Marine Disaster

THE TORONTO DAILY STAR

WANT AD AND REAL ESTATE MEDIUM
The Star Delivers "The Goods"

20TH YEAR   TORONTO, FRIDAY, APRIL 19, 1912—THIRTY-TWO PAGES.   Last Edition.   ONE CENT.

BRAVE MEN ON SS. TITANIC SMILED IN FACE OF DEATH

HUSBANDS WAVED HANDS AS WIVES AND CHILDREN ROWED AWAY INTO DARKNESS FROM THE SHIP

The Toronto Star, April 19, 1912

In the early hours of April 15, 1912, the *Titanic* hit an iceberg off the coast of Newfoundland and sank. Of the 2,223 people aboard the ship, 832 passengers and 685 crew members died.

Since the sinking of the *Titanic* in April 1912, stricter measures had been adopted to keep passengers safe at sea. Ships had to carry enough lifeboats to hold all aboard, in case tragedy struck. As a result, the *Empress* counted enough lifeboats and life jackets for all the passengers and crew the liner could accommodate.

Although the *Empress* was a safe ship, the crippling patches of fog that often blanketed the waters of the St. Lawrence River would soon seal her fate.

PASSENGER CHRONICLES

Jenny Livelton

Jenny Livelton grew up in Bardu, Norway, where she went to school and worked with her parents and 12 brothers and sisters on their small farm. Cattle, goats, and sheep, along with grain and garden vegetables, supplied the family with food and clothing. But life was hard, so when news came of a faraway place promising free land for the taking, the temptation to leave Norway became irresistible. Her two older brothers, John and Bernhard, were the first to go. The rest of the family soon followed, sailing to Canada on the *Empress* in July 1913, when Jenny was 20 years old.

Jennie Livelton (standing at back) and her family.

After reaching Quebec, the family first travelled by train to Edson, Alberta. That winter, once they had secured a piece of land, they followed a route called the "ice highway" to Grande Prairie to build their homestead. For six weeks the Liveltons trudged over frozen lakes and rivers in sleighs pulled by horses and oxen. A few cows travelled with the family, to provide milk during the journey.

Merlin Huth

The youngest of four boys and three girls, Merlin Huth and his siblings, Lancelot, Galahad, Enid, Vivien, Elaine, and Frances, were all named after characters in the

Robin Huth Collection

story of King Arthur and the Knights of the Round Table. In his late teens, Merlin left his native England to become a shepherd in New Zealand, on a ranch belonging to his brother, Lancelot. When he tired of that he sailed to Canada in search of adventure. He had planned to sail on the *Titanic*, but cancelled his reservation when he learned there were no more first-class tickets available. Merlin arrived in Saint John, New Brunswick, on the *Empress of Ireland* on April 13, 1912, two days before the *Titanic* sank.

Merlin Huth.

He settled in Salmon Arm, British Columbia, where he bought a large piece of land to grow apples on. But he had barely finished planting his orchard when the First World War broke out. Merlin crossed the Atlantic once again and served as a lieutenant in the Imperial Camel Corps in Egypt, at times helping Lawrence of Arabia to dismantle enemy communications. When the war was over, Merlin returned to Salmon Arm, where he married and raised two children.

Ron and Maureen Venzi Collection

Edith Mary Oxley Jackson.

Edith Mary Oxley Jackson

Edith Mary Oxley was born into a middle-class family in Yorkshire, England, in 1860. Orphaned by the age of 20, she went to live in Liverpool with an aunt who helped her find employment as a housekeeper for Richard Jackson, a respectable widower with four children. The housekeeping arrangement led to marriage in 1885, and Edith Mary and Richard had two more children. When her husband's business failed in the early 1900s, the family decided to move to Canada. They sold everything and sailed in October 1911, aboard the *Empress of Ireland*.

They settled in South Vancouver, British Columbia, where they cleared their land and built a home with comforts such as running hot water. Although the isolated, rugged farming life was very different from the bustling city environment of Liverpool, the family adapted well to their new life. In later years, after the death of her husband, Edith Mary moved with two of her children to Montague Harbour on Galiano Island, where they operated a rustic summer lodge.

Joyce Thompson Gould

Five-year-old Joyce Thompson sailed aboard the *Empress of Ireland* on May 3, 1912, with her mother and three siblings. Originally from Sussex, England, the family was on their way to Canada to join her father, Charlie, who had immigrated a year earlier and found a job in Edmonton, Alberta.

During the crossing, Joyce went up on deck every day and watched the foamy track the ship left behind. One day Joyce asked one of the ship's crew, a cabin boy, what everyone was looking for as they gazed out to sea. "Icebergs, of course," he said. But Joyce understood "ice birds," so she asked the cabin boy what he did when he caught them, to which he answered, "I crush them

Joyce Thompson Gould Collection

Joyce Gould, at right, with her sister Margaret.

up and make ice cream." When Joyce ate ice cream later that day, she looked carefully to see if there were any feathers in her dessert.

Joyce eventually settled in Rosalind, Alberta, where she married Duff Gould. She lived a long life as a farmer's wife, mother, teacher, and poet, and took university courses well into her 70s.

James Turnbull Cornthwaite

When the *Empress of Ireland* sailed from Liverpool for Quebec on October 3, 1913, it was carrying 1,473 passengers. Among them were Margaret Cornthwaite of Manchester, England, and her four children. Pregnant with their fifth child, Margaret was relieved that her husband William had been able to send her enough money for them to sail before the new baby was born. William Cornthwaite had travelled to Canada a few months earlier in search of work and was now employed as a miner in Sudbury, Ontario, where he eagerly awaited a reunion with his family.

James Turnbull Cornthwaite at 18 years old.

Gordon Cornthwaite Collection

Perhaps it was the rocking of the ship that brought on the events of October 5, for when the *Empress* docked in Quebec on October 10, it counted one more passenger. William Cornthwaite greeted not five, but six members of his family. The baby boy was named James Turnbull Cornthwaite, after the ship's captain, James Turnbull, who was making his first voyage in command of the *Empress of Ireland*.

THE LAST GOODBYE

With the St. Lawrence River no longer sheathed in ice, the *Empress* took up her summer route and sailed from Liverpool for Quebec on May 15, 1914. On May 22, she made one of her occasional stops off Grosse Île, so a family with scarlet fever could be quarantined. She then continued on to Quebec, where she arrived in port at 2:30 that afternoon, with her remaining 1,169 passengers.

For the following six days, the *Empress* was readied for her return crossing to Liverpool. During this time, 1,100 tons of cargo and passengers' luggage were loaded onto the ship, along with more than 2,400 tons of coal needed to power her back across the Atlantic. By early afternoon on May 28, 1914, the liner's 432 crew members and 1,057 passengers had made their way up the gangways, and many were now pressed against the ship's railings, waving to family and friends who had come to see them off.

The ship's 87 first-class passengers, largely made up of rich families, business leaders, and high-ranking government officials, also included British actors Laurence Irving and his wife Mabel Hackney, hunter and explorer Sir Henry Seton-Karr, and insect specialist Henry Herbert Lyman. The second- and third-class passengers included more than 150 members of the Canadian Salvation Army, who were off to attend the organization's Third International Congress in London, as well as working-class immigrants returning to their homelands to visit relatives.

Luggage inspection aboard the Empress.

David St-Pierre Collection

David St-Pierre Collection

Actors Laurence Irving and Mabel Hackney.

Members of the Salvation Army aboard the *Empress*.

TIME CAPSULE

The Salvation Army is a charitable and religious organization that was founded in London, England, in 1865 to care for the poor and homeless. Structured like an army, its members have ranks and wear uniforms, as they do in the military.

Salvation Army Canadian Staff Band.

At 4:30 p.m., the *Empress* threw off her moorings and began her slow glide down the St. Lawrence River, under the command of Captain Henry George Kendall.

The *Empress* leaving the Port of Quebec City on her last voyage.

The ship's last crossing of the Atlantic had begun.

The calm, clear night held the promise of an uneventful journey. By 10:00 p.m., many of the ship's passengers had retired to their cabins and were readying themselves for bed. Around 12:50 a.m., the steamer *Lady Evelyn* met the *Empress* off Rimouski for the usual exchange of mailbags. Letters and postcards written by passengers during their short journey from Quebec City were unloaded onto the steamer, while mailbags destined for England were loaded onto the *Empress*. A half-hour later, the pilot boat *Eureka* met the *Empress* to collect the river pilot and drop him off at Pointe-au-Père.

At approximately 1:40 a.m. on May 29, the *Empress*'s lookout reported an incoming ship about 10 kilometres off the right side of the liner. The ship was the Norwegian collier *Storstad*, on its way to Montreal to deliver its cargo of 10,400 tons of coal.

As the two ships approached one another, a patch of fog suddenly crept across the river. First it blanketed the *Storstad*, then the *Empress*.

Now blinded by the heavy mist, the two ships exchanged horn signals to alert each other of their positions and courses. Tragically, these were misunderstood. While Captain Kendall and his crew took actions for the *Empress* to pass the *Storstad* starboard-to-starboard, or right-side-to-right side, the crew of the *Storstad* altered the collier's route for the ships to pass port-to-port, or left-side-to-left-side.

Then, it happened.

At 1:55 a.m., the *Storstad* loomed out of the thick fog heading straight for the *Empress*. Despite being much smaller than the liner, the *Storstad* had a reinforced bow to push aside the ice on the St. Lawrence during the late fall and early spring months. Barely a jolt was felt aboard the *Empress* as the *Storstad* sliced five and a half metres deep into the ship's starboard side.

With the collier now embedded perpendicularly into the *Empress*, and only six kilometres from land, Captain Kendall tried to beach the liner on the river's south shore. But the forward motion of the *Empress* prevented the *Storstad* from staying where she was and keeping the tear in the liner's side sealed. Instead, the collier was wrenched out of the liner, leaving behind a gigantic gash more than eight metres high and four metres wide, through which over 200,000 litres of water poured in every second. Within minutes of the blow, the *Empress* began listing to starboard.

Rushing water also flooded into the ship through open portholes on the lower decks, drowning many people in their beds.

Because they had only been at sea for a few hours, most passengers were unfamiliar with the ship's layout and scrambled to find their life jackets and make their way to

The *Empress of Ireland* is struck amidships by the collier *Storstad*. *The Sphere*, June 6, 1914.

The difficulty of the stairs and the dark. *Illustrated London News*, June 13, 1914.

the upper decks. Captain Kendall ordered the stewards to awaken sleeping passengers and ready the lifeboats for launching. But because of her perilous list to starboard, no lifeboats on the *Empress*'s left side could be lowered, and only a few on her right side ever made it into the water.

Within six minutes the *Empress*'s engine room was flooded and her electrical power began to fail. The ship's telegraph operator sent out what would be the *Empress*'s only SOS message. Then the lights went out.

TIME CAPSULE

William Clark cheated death for the second time when he survived the sinking of the *Empress*. Two years earlier, in 1912, Clark was working aboard the *Titanic* as a stoker when she hit an iceberg and sank off the coast of Newfoundland. Although they worked in the deepest parts of ships, stokers and engineers often survived shipwrecks. In the case of the *Empress*, they were first to know the ship was doomed when the boiler rooms had flooded. They were also among the first to be released from duty and had direct access to the boat decks, by way of ladders that ran directly from the engine rooms to the highest deck, just at the bottom of the funnel near the ship's stern.

TIME CAPSULE

The Empress was built according to the two-compartment rule. This meant the ship should be able to stay afloat even if two of her 11 compartments were flooded. However, the *Empress*'s most vulnerable areas were her middle compartments, where the boiler rooms and engine rooms were located. These were the first two compartments to be flooded when the *Storstad* struck. This resulted in the *Empress* losing her electricity and power within minutes of the collision. Also, to keep the other compartments from flooding, the watertight doors between them had to be closed. Because the *Empress* began listing so quickly, the crew was unable to shut these doors, and the remaining compartments flooded one after the other.

PASSENGER CHRONICLES

William Hird

William Hird celebrated his 16th birthday on the wharf at Quebec City, only six days before the *Empress* set out on her last crossing. William had been working on ships to support his family ever since his father died when he was 13, and the *Empress* was his first big ship. He worked as a steward on the liner and took care of the ship's engineers by making their beds and bringing them their meals. Shortly after the *Storstad* struck the *Empress*, William was startled awake by one of the stewards with whom he shared living quarters. While the other terrified stewards scurried to get dressed, William quickly pulled on a pair of pants and a jacket and made his way to the upper decks of the ship. He then dove into the river and swam with difficulty towards one of the *Storstad*'s lifeboats. Once aboard the coal ship he was given a hot drink and dry clothes. Following the sinking of the *Empress*, William returned to his family in Liverpool, England, and served in the merchant marine during the First World War. He then married and moved to Australia, where he raised his six children and lived out the remainder of his life until his death at age 85.

Marjorie Hird Collection

William Hird, at left, with his mother and younger siblings, circa 1912.

Dr. James F. Grant

The *Empress* had already lost electrical power when 23-year-old James F. Grant was rolled out of his berth by the listing of the ship. A 1913 graduate of McGill University, James had only recently joined the crew of the *Empress* as the ship's doctor. Struggling to make his way outside, he crawled on his hands and knees, following the trail of tack nails that held down the carpet. After he was pulled through a porthole by fellow passengers, he slid into the freezing water as the liner sank from beneath him. The young doctor swam towards the lights of the *Storstad* and was soon picked up by one of the collier's lifeboats. He immediately set to work

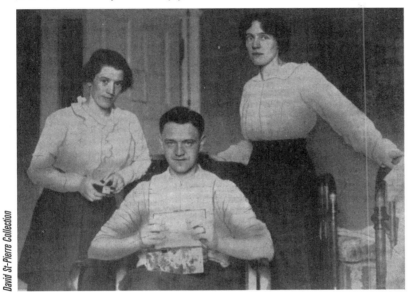

David St-Pierre Collection

Dr. Grant with two nurses, following the wreck.

helping save other passengers. Later, aboard the *Storstad*, James tirelessly calmed and tended to the terror-stricken passengers, many with broken limbs or near death from the cold. He was later praised by surviving passengers as a hero.

AFTERMATH

In the inky darkness, hundreds of people, including Captain Kendall, were thrown into the near-freezing waters of the St. Lawrence River as the *Empress* tilted farther right, until both her funnels slapped the water.

As for the *Storstad*, she had suffered severe injury to her bow but was otherwise undamaged by the collision. On board, the ship's captain, Thomas Andersen, and his crew were unaware of the plight of the *Empress*. No longer able to see the liner, they assumed she had only suffered minor damage and had continued on her course. But the cries for help, which soon began to rise from the water, alerted them to the fate of the doomed ship.

Immediately, crew members launched all the *Storstad*'s lifeboats and feverishly began rescue efforts.

As passengers struggled to keep afloat by clutching at deck chairs, furniture, and other debris from the ship, Captain Kendall was plucked from the waters and hauled aboard one of the few *Empress* lifeboats that had been successfully lowered into the water. He quickly set to work wrenching others from the river's icy grasp. Once the lifeboat was filled to capacity, it painstakingly made its way toward the *Storstad*, with several freezing passengers hanging from its sides.

Passengers standing on the side of the *Empress of Ireland* just before she sank. *The Sphere*, June 6, 1914.

Courtesy of the National Library of Ireland

Once aboard the collier, the rescued passengers were rushed to the engine and boiler rooms to warm themselves by the furnaces. *Storstad* crew members also used any material they could find — including tablecloths, curtains, and their own clothing — to cover the shivering survivors, most of whom were only partially clothed or in pyjamas.

David St-Pierre Collection

Captain Andersen.

At 2:09 a.m., 14 minutes after the moment of impact, the *Empress* rested almost flat on her right side in the water. The river then swallowed her up.

Damage to *Storstad* caused by collision with the *Empress of Ireland*.

Twelve kilometres upriver, the Marconi station at Pointe-au-Père had received the *Empress*'s SOS message. The *Eureka*, which less than an hour earlier had collected the pilot from the *Empress*, raced towards the wreck site. The *Lady Evelyn*, which had collected the mail off Rimouski, was also dispatched. Crew members aboard both steamers met with a dismal sight. Few passengers remained alive in the frigid waters, having by then died of hypothermia. Joining the *Storstad* in its rescue efforts, the crews of the *Lady Evelyn* and *Eureka* continued to scan the river's surface for signs of life.

Men of the *Storstad*'s crew.

By 3:00 a.m., cries were no longer heard and only floating corpses could be found.

Survivors and the bodies of dead passengers were transferred from the *Storstad* onto the steamers *Eureka* and *Lady Evelyn* and taken to Rimouski, where stunned townspeople were waking to the horrifying news. They quickly opened their homes and shops to provide clothing, food, and supplies to the rescued.

Later, a train carried survivors to Quebec, where those requiring urgent medical attention were rushed to the hospital, and the slightly injured were given rooms at the Chateau Frontenac Hotel.

Survivors of the *Empress* boarding a special train at Rimouski.

It was not long before news of the sinking made its way across Canada and beyond. Outside the Canadian Pacific Railway offices in London, hundreds of people gathered, waiting for the lists of survivors to be posted. In the end, the death toll was staggering. A total of 1,012 people — 172 crew members and 840 passengers — had perished, 134 of them children.

Quebec Chronicle, May 30, 1914.

Toronto Daily Star, May 30, 1914.

On the last day of May, the steamer *Lady Grey* left Rimouski for Quebec City. Lined up on her deck were the caskets of 188 passengers who had been pulled from the river or had washed up on shore. In Quebec, Pier 27 was converted into a morgue where relatives of those who drowned had the heartbreaking task of identifying their bodies. Within a week, funerals were being held across Canada to bury the dead.

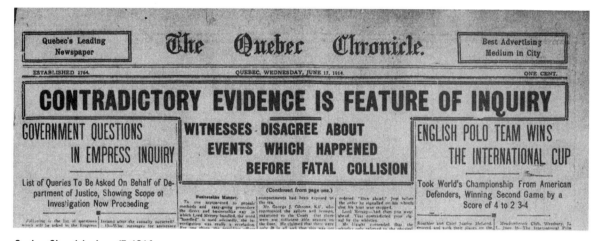

Quebec Chronicle, June 17, 1914.

The inquiry to investigate the cause of the disaster began on June 16 in Quebec City. It lasted 12 days, during which time 62 witnesses were asked more than 8,000 questions.

Finally, despite contradictory testimonies given by crew members from both the *Empress* and the *Storstad*, which left no clear picture of what had really happened under the blanket of fog, a decision was rendered. The fault, it was determined, rested with the *Storstad*.

PASSENGER CHRONICLES

Arthur James Blackham

Arthur James Blackham and his fiancée Ethel Hill looked forward to marrying and building a life together. In 1911, Arthur left Ethel behind in their native town of Peterborough, England, and sailed to Canada to find work to support himself and his future wife. He joined his older sister and her husband, who had immigrated to Canada a few years earlier and were living in Wilmot, Ontario. Arthur worked as

a conductor for Toronto's tramway system, and by 1914 had earned enough money for he and Ethel to marry. In the spring, Arthur booked passage back to England on the *Empress* to collect his fiancée. The couple planned to return to Canada and settle down. Sadly, Ethel and Arthur were never married, as he was one of the 717 third-class passengers who died on May 29.

Family photo of 18-year-old Arthur James Blackham, in 1907: left to right, Father John Blackham, Arthur Blackham (at the back), sisters Alice Ethel Blackham and Agnes Ann Blackham, brother John Christopher William, and mother Agnes Levina Blackham.

Alma Fedora Maud Assafrey

The youngest of six daughters, Alma Fedora Maud Assafrey was born in 1887 in Glasgow, Scotland. Her Russian father was a prosperous restaurateur and candy-maker who became famous for his toffee and for opening Scotland's first chocolate factory. Gifted and independent, Alma studied at the Glasgow School of Art, where one of her teachers was Alexander J. Musgrove. When Alexander was appointed as first

principal of the new Winnipeg School of Art, the couple became engaged. Alexander sailed to Canada in June 1913 while Alma continued to teach at a girls' school in Helensburgh, Scotland. The following spring, she joined Alexander. Only weeks after her arrival in Winnipeg, Alma realized that she could not adapt to the difficult conditions of frontier life in Manitoba and decided to return to her native Scotland. She booked a second-class passage on the *Empress of Ireland* and perished in the wreck.

Valentine Rodger Collection

Alma Fedora Maud Assafrey.

90

Marcus and Elisabet Katarina Blomquist

When the *Virginian* sailed from Liverpool on March 29, 1912, her passengers included the Swedish immigrants Marcus and Elisabet Katarina Blomquist and their seven sons and two daughters. Arriving in Halifax, Nova Scotia, on April 6, the family boarded a train for western Canada. Their final destination was Hayter, Alberta, where they joined the oldest son, John, on the farm he had purchased when he first immigrated to Canada in 1906. While the older Blomquist children settled and became farmers, Marcus and Elisabet Katarina missed their native homeland and grew unhappy with their life in Canada. In the spring of 1914, the couple decided to return to Sweden with their two youngest sons, Olov Sigfrid, age 11, and Erik Walfrid, age nine. All four perished when the *Empress of Ireland* sank. Their bodies were never identified and are believed to have been buried in a mass grave in Rimouski.

Blomquist family.

Irene Johnstone Collection

91

Major David Creighton and Bertha Creighton

On May 27, Major David Creighton and Bertha Creighton kissed their five children goodbye in Toronto. They travelled by train to Quebec City, where they joined more than 150 other Salvation Army members aboard the *Empress*. Sadly, only 29 of their group survived. The bodies of Major and Bertha Creighton were never recovered. A few days after learning they were orphans, the five Creighton children were surprised to receive two letters, one from their mother and the other from their father. Bertha had written her letter on the train from Toronto to Quebec, while Major Creighton had written his shortly after boarding the *Empress*. The letters had then been unloaded off Rimouski, less than an hour and a half before the *Storstad* struck the liner. Because the older children were unable to care for their younger siblings, the family was split up. Relatives took in the two youngest children; four-year-old Cyrus was sent to Alberta while eight-year-old Arthur went to New Brunswick. Despite the great distances that separated them, all five children remained in close contact with each other as they grew up.

David Creighton Collection

Bottom row, left to right: Mrs. Bertha Creighton, Arthur, Cyrus, and Major David Creighton. Top row, left to right: Older children Wilfred, Edna, and Will.

Henry Herbert Lyman

From early childhood Henry Herbert Lyman loved insects, and he spent his life putting together a collection of bugs of all kinds. On May 28, he and his wife set off for England aboard the *Empress* for their postponed honeymoon. Neither survived. In his will, Henry Lyman gave his insect collection, consisting of approximately 20,000 specimens, to McGill University. It became the foundation of the university's Lyman Entomological Museum and Research Laboratory

Courtesy of the Lyman Entomological Museum and Research Laboratory

Henry Herbert Lyman.

LEGACY

In the weeks following the loss of the *Empress of Ireland*, efforts were made to retrieve the ship's "treasure" of 212 bars of silver destined for London, numerous bags of mail, as well as the Purser's safe. But the dark underwater world of the ship's interior was almost impossible for the divers to navigate due to their cumbersome diving suits and the river's frigid waters and strong currents. Dynamite was used to blast a hole on the ship's side through which the Purser's safe was eventually hoisted to the surface on August 20, 1914. Two days later, it was opened to reveal a small amount of cash and travellers' cheques, which were returned to surviving passengers or family members of the deceased.

During the course of that summer, the rumblings of war in Europe had grown increasingly loud. After Germany declared war against Russia on August 1, igniting the First World War, death tolls from the battlefields of Europe soon vastly outnumbered the death toll of the lost liner. Newspaper headlines screamed the devastation of war and, within months, the tragic story of the *Empress of Ireland* faded from people's minds and slipped into history.

Silver bars salvaged from the wreck.

Site historique maritime de la Pointe-au-Père Collection

The Purser's safe, in which passengers' money, jewels, documents, and other valuables were stored for safekeeping during each crossing.

Site historique maritime de la Pointe-au-Père Collection

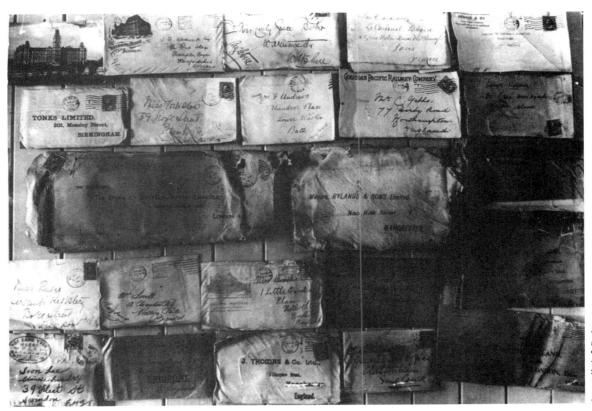

Over 20,000 letters were recovered from the *Empress*. After each piece of mail had dried, it was stamped "Recovered by Divers from Wreck of S.S. *Empress of Ireland*" and returned to its sender, if the address was still legible.

Site historique maritime de la Pointe-au-Père Collection

Each diver was dressed in a rubber and canvas suit, weighted boots, a breastplate, and a copper helmet, which was bolted to their outfit. Air was pumped to the diver from the surface through a hose.

Divers ready for salvage operation.

Site historique maritime de la Pointe-au-Père Collection

For fifty years, the *Empress of Ireland* lay undisturbed, washed by the currents of the St. Lawrence River, until she was rediscovered in July 1964 by a team of divers. The wreck soon became a popular diving site. As a result, many artifacts, including dishes, utensils, pieces of furniture, and passengers' belongings, were taken from the site.

In 1980, some of the divers who had removed artifacts helped create a museum in Pointe-au-Père, called the Musée de la mer, to display the objects they had collected. This museum now houses the largest collection of *Empress of Ireland* artifacts in the world.

TIME CAPSULE

Following the sinking of the *Empress of Ireland*, both Captain Andersen and Captain Kendall survived torpedo attacks by German U-boats off the coast of Ireland during the First World War. Captain Andersen was commanding the *Storstad*, to which he had been re-assigned after she was repaired, when the ship was torpedoed in March 1917. A year later, in March 1918, Captain Kendall was second-in-command of a passenger liner, the *Calgarian*, when it came under attack. It took four torpedoes to sink the ship, which went down with 49 crew members.

In recognition of the greatest maritime tragedy in Canada's peacetime history, and to prevent further scavenging, the wreck of the *Empress* was declared a historical and archeological site by the Quebec government in April 1999. Every spring a buoy is floated above the site to mark its location and to remind divers that it is strictly forbidden to remove artifacts or to tamper with the wreck in any way.

A decade later, in 2009, the wreck was designated a national historic site by the Historic Sites and Monuments Board of Canada.

Today, the *Empress of Ireland* still rests on her starboard side at a depth of approximately 42 metres. Bathed in the underwater world of the St. Lawrence, she appears to be almost sinking into the floor of the river.

Site historique maritime de la Pointe-au-Père Collection

Bugle salvaged from the wreck.

Langis Dubé Collection

China pitcher salvaged from the wreck. Dish patterns for first- and second-class passengers were more ornate than those of third-class passengers.

Site historique maritime de la Pointe-au-Père Collection

One of the wheels salvaged from the wreck.

Claude Villeneuve Collection

First-class sign salvaged from the wreck.

But her story is far from over. Her legacy continues to be carried forward by the descendants of the thousands of newcomers who chose to make Canada their adoptive country at the start of the twentieth century. They are living reminders of the important role the proud liner played in the history of Canada.

Empress of Ireland Pavillon (formerly called Musée de la mer) at Pointe-au-Père.

Culture et Communication Québec

A buoy is placed above the wreck every spring to indicate that it is a protected site.

TIME CAPSULE

Today, Canada counts approximately one million descendants of immigrants who sailed aboard the *Empress of Ireland* between 1906 and 1914, seeking better opportunities for themselves and their children.

LEXICON

Artifact:	An object from a particular period in human history.
Bow:	The front end of a ship, usually pointed.
Cabin boy:	A boy servant aboard a ship who takes cares of officers and passengers.
Collier:	A cargo ship designed to carry coal.
Deck:	A floor or level on a ship.
Edwardian Era:	The period in British history when Edward VII was king, from 1901 to 1910.
Galley:	The kitchen on a ship.
Helm:	The mechanism used to steer a ship.
Hypothermia:	A life-threatening condition that occurs when the temperature of the body becomes abnormally low because it has been exposed to cold water or cold air for too long.
Immigrants:	People who move from one country, usually their homeland, to live permanently in another country.

Keel: The keel is the first part of the ship to be built and serves as its foundation. It is the spine of the ship and runs along its bottom, supporting the structure above.

Knot: Speed in water is measured in knots. One knot is 1.852 kilometres per hour.

Life jackets: Vests worn to keep people afloat in the water.

List: When a ship leans or tilts to one side it is said to be listing.

Moorings: Fixed objects on a dock or pier to which a ship is tied when it is in port.

Port side: The left-hand side of a ship, when you are standing on deck facing the bow.

Scullions: People who work in a kitchen, where they perform tasks like washing dishes.

Settlers: Settlers are immigrants who leave their country or geographic area and move to another country or area to live and cultivate the land.

Starboard side: The right-hand side of a ship, when you are standing on deck facing the bow.

Stern: The back end of a ship.

Torpedo: An explosive weapon launched underwater to sink ships. U-boats and other warships fire torpedoes.

U-boat: Shortened version of *Unterseeboot* (under the sea boat), which means "submarine" in German.

TIMELINE

1867 — New Brunswick, Nova Scotia, Ontario, and Quebec are united to create the Dominion of Canada

1870 — Manitoba and the Northwest Territories join Canada

1871 — British Columbia joins Canada

1873 — Prince Edward Island joins Canada

1881 — Canadian Pacific Railway is founded

1885 — Last spike is driven into the last rail of the Canadian Pacific Railway

1898 — The Yukon Territory joins Canada

1904 — Canadian Pacific Railway places its order with the Fairfield Shipbuilding and Engineering Company to build the Atlantic *Empresses*

1905 — Alberta and Saskatchewan join Canada

1906 — Maiden voyage of the *Empress of Ireland*

1912 — *Titanic* sinks on her maiden voyage on April 15

1914 — *Empress of Ireland* sinks on May 29

1914–18 — The First World War

1964 — Wreck of the *Empress of Ireland* is rediscovered by divers

1980 — Musée de la mer opens in Pointe-au-Père, Quebec

1999 — Wreck of the *Empress of Ireland* is declared an historic site by the province of Quebec

2009 — Wreck of the *Empress of Ireland* is declared a National Historic Site by the Historic Sites and Monuments Board of Canada

FURTHER READING

Adams, Simon. *Eyewitness: Titanic*. Toronto: Dorling Kindersley Ltd., 2009.

Ballard, Robert, Rick Archbold, Ken Marschall. *Lost Liners*. New York: Hyperion Books, 1997.

Creighton, David. *Losing the Empress: A Personal Journey*. Toronto: Dundurn Press, 2000.

Croall, James. *Fourteen Minutes: Last Voyage of the Empress of Ireland*. London: Sphere, 1980.

Grout, Derek. *Empress of Ireland: The Story of an Edwardian Liner*. Stroud, U.K.: Tempus Publishing Ltd., 2002.

Renaud, Anne. *Island of Hope and Sorrow: The Story of Gross Île*. Montreal: Lobster Press, 2007.

Renaud, Anne. *Pier 21: Stories From Near and Far*. Montreal: Lobster Press, 2008.

Temple, Bob. *The Titanic: An Interactive History Adventure*. Mankato, MN: Capstone Press, 2008.

Thompson, Alexa, Debi Van de Wiel. *Pier 21: An Illustrated History of Canada's Gateway*. Halifax: Nimbus Publishing, 2002.

Zeni, David. *Forgotten Empress: The Empress of Ireland Story*. Fredericton: Goose Lane Editions, 1998.

Losing the Empress
A Personal Journey
David Creighton
978-1550023404
$22.99

The *Empress of Ireland's* last voyage ended on May 29, 1914, when she was rammed by a Norwegian coal-carrier in a fog patch on the St. Lawrence River near Rimouski. For David Creighton, her voyage still continues.

In *Losing the Empress*, Creighton delves into the lives of his grandparents — Salvation Army officers who were lost on the Empress — and the lives of their five orphaned children who would soon be plunged into the First World War. His discoveries reveal amazing details about the *Empress*, which sank in fourteen minutes with a greater loss of life than the *Titanic* disaster.

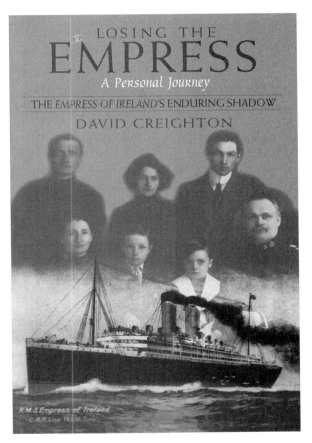